Feelings

M H

India | USA | UK

Presentation by *BookLeaf Publishing*

Web: www.bookleafpub.com

E-mail: info@bookleafpub.com

ISBN: 9789358313321

First edition 2023

DEDICATION

To 🌸 you, my weird connection ! Thank you for allowing me to express myself in ways that weren't comfortable for you. For me it meant my life.

The beginning

Oh night you came to me so soon
I'm not ready so please take a turn
I feel the dark behind the stars
Please let the moon to show her lights

Feelings rising

The leaves are falling
The wind is blowing
The dark is coming
No sign of turning
Squeeze tight
to make it right
No air to leak around
Not a word to come out
There's ways to feel
The choice is real
Squeeze it strong
To feel the numb
The leaves are down
The wind is gone
The dark is on
No turn around

Shhh... shhh

Shhh... shhh...
Don't cry
Your not worthy
To cry

Shhh... shhh...
Don't talk
Your not worthy
To talk

Shhh... shhh...
Don't live
Your not worthy
To live

Shhh... shhh.
Don't die
Your not worthy
To die

Shhh... shhh...
Feel the pain
Your worthy
To feel the pain .

Let it roll

I know I shouldn't
I know I should stay here
I'm weak
I'll just let it roll

My night is long
My body is numb
My tears are burning down my cheeks
My heart is slowing down from beat
My breathe is gone
And so I wish
My arms are strong
I feel the squeeze
I see you watch
I close my eyes
I care to much

On my mind

And you're on my mind
How can I see the light
When you don't seem to mind
My eyes are closed
They hurt to much
The shadows are closed
No dark is to much
I try to be
For you to see
My best of me
How could I be
I feel the hope
Is next to me
I burn the rope
For no one to see
It's already night
You're still on my mind
I need to fight
You still don't mind

Another world

6

Another world is rising
I feel each stone , one by one
Laying down through my ribs
A castle shape is done
And all the lights are gone.
I see how trapped I feel
And all alone inside I kneel

Who are you ?

Who are you
You're just the forests that knows my thoughts
Who are you
You're just the rivers that carries my feelings
Who are you
You're just the falls that crushes my hopes
Who are you
You're just the shadows that reveals my form
Who are you
Because Your actions shutters my heart

Later

Please open your eyes
Sooner than later
Please open your mind
Sooner than later
To listen to my heart
Sooner than later

Don't close your eyes
Not now not later
Don't shut your mind
Not now not later
To see my truth
Sooner than later

Touch in ways

You touch my soul
In so many ways
I see my needs
To break in layers

You touch my heart
Every time you write
I feel my blood
it's coming alive

You touch my spirit
When you're connected
I need to keep it
But you quickly disconnect

You touch my mind
In a lot of ways
I want to stay
But you're pushing me away.

Need to breathe

I feel the struggles inside me
I feel the bubbles boiling in
I feel the pain my heart endure
I need to breathe.

One day

If only you would understand
If only you would try
If only you would see the truth
If only you would see my eyes
If only you wouldn't hurt me anymore.

One day

Don't close your eyes

12

I can't breathe it's too hard
I want a hand right on my head

I feel the pins right in my skin
I see the blood that leaves my arm

Don't close your eyes
The pain is mine

Hold

13

Come, hold my hand
I know it's cold
Come on!
The blood is warm
I know you can't
You hate the blood
The blood is meant
Your hate, I feel

What's done is done
I can't undo
I feel so strange
I Cannot see

Beg to breathe

14

I beg the universe
for no one to feel
Fated to feel.
For no one to need
someone's actions
to be able to breathe .

Inhumane

15

I feel so cold after this day
I froze in instant all the way
I never thought you have the guts
To be inhumane in your thoughts .

I know this words are harsh today
I wish you'll never do a yesterday
To feel the coldness in the veins
That's everything that I have left .

My angel

I close my eyes
To meet my angel
She flown away
Apart of me

I close my eyes
To meet my grief
She's here
In a darker fit

I close my eyes
To meet my tears
They run away
Into my cheeks

I close my eye's
To meet and feel
My heart
To beat or not to beat .

Pieces to care

So many pieces on the floor
So many of them without color
I'm lost in finding just my own
To bad I'm all alone
I ask for help to keep my own
I realize I'm all alone.
No human is here to care
Not even me can justify the care

Fated to feel

Feted to feel I called myself
When light is pushing me so far away
I'm cursed to feel in any way
The thoughts are rolling in their way

Fated to feel I called my self
When dark is taking me away
I'm cursed to feel in any way
The pain is making her on way

www.ingramcontent.com/pod-product-compliance
Lightning Source LLC
LaVergne TN
LVHW050311210726
843507LV00020B/3106